Dap… …ch
than…
for your …
& support
…

THE GREAT BRITISH POETS

VOLUME XVIII: MIKE O'BRIEN

ISBN-13: 978-1500803711
ISBN-10: 1500803715

To Judy

Living with a creative genius can’t always be easy.

CONTENTS

ACKNOWLEDGMENTS

I owe a debt of gratitude to all who have inspired and encouraged me, from Mr William "Killer" Kennedy, my form tutor at Wilberforce Junior High School in Hull, through to the excellent Pitmen Poets of Mexborough, the Rotherham Open Mic Poets (ROMP) and associated organizations in South Yorkshire and beyond.

FOREWORD

By Professor Iain Duncan Norville, Chair of English Literature, the University of Wath upon Dearne

When I was asked to write the forward to this volume of "The Great British Poets," My first reaction was one of unadulterated joy. It is not often that I get asked to write an introduction to anything these days. That sort of work seems to be farmed out to more fashionable types than myself, and even if they are chairs of literature in some university or another, one normally discovers that they have also spent time performing in a pop group or making a television programme in which they travel the world smiling at the camera and having interesting conversations with people that they meet.

That could have been me. If it wasn't for the facial disfigurement and the resultant speech impediment. Curse that tin of jam sponge. If I were to give you one piece of advice, just one thing to take away from the preface of this book, it would be this: "To prevent spurting, hold cloth over can when removing top" Being squirted with boiling hot jam is no laughing matter.

But all that is beside the point. My first reaction of unmitigated joy was quickly replaced by one of fear and trepidation. (I am now talking about being asked to write this foreword, not my accident with the tinned sponge.) Who was, or is Mike O'Brien, and what poetry has he written?

After availing myself of the resources of the University Library, I was still none the wiser. A period of Internet research was fruitful, but threw up rather too many Mike O'Brien's to be of much use.

Apparently the man who took off all his clothes and ran across the pitch at Twickenham when England were playing France in 1974 was called Mike O'Brien, but he has never published a poem in his life. There was another Mike O'Brien who held several Ministerial posts in Tony

Blair's Labour Government, and yet another one who appears on an American television programme called "Saturday Night Live" performing humorous pieces with titles such as "Mike O'Brien Would Like to Kiss You" and "Seven Minutes in Heaven" One wonders whether kissing this particular Mike O'Brien would transport a person to heaven for seven minutes, but as a largely heterosexual man, I don't dwell too much on such reveries.

Another Mike O'Brien failed to make a dent in the pop charts with a recording called "Made in Germany" in the late 1970s, despite being on the Stiff label, which launched the careers of such great British poets as Ian Dury, Elvis Costello and Suggs out of Madness. Again, this is not the Mike O'Brien who is the subject of this volume of mediocre poetry.

Neither is he the Mike O'Brien I found who has released a string of albums over the past ten years or so, which appear to be of the genre "Christian Rock." After listening to his appalling single "Wishing Well" I began to despair of ever finding the Mike O'Brien in question, and more importantly, of ever claiming my fee for writing his introduction.

Facebook is a complete sea of Mike O'Briens "Pennsylvania State Representative Mike O'Brien," "Mike O'Brien AKA Guitar Mike Rocks," "Mike O'Brien Bass Guitar/ Vocalist at The Sweet Blues Band" One who introduces himself: "My name is Mike O'Brien and I am running for Congress to represent the people of Michigan's Sixth District." There are so many to choose from.

In desperation, I turned to the commissioning letter. Amazingly, it was from Mike O'Brien himself, and contained details of where I could find his biography and examples of his poetry. If I were to give you one more piece of advice, just one more thing to take away from the preface of this book, it would be this: When you receive a written communication, read the damn thing properly.

You may save yourself a lot of time.

So then…

The Mike O'Brien whose works are featured in this slim volume is NOT a Great British Poet. Not by any standard of judgment as far as I can see. He may be British. He may lay claim to being a poet, in that he has written some poetry, of sorts. But his poetry certainly is not great. As you will no doubt discover as you leaf through the works on offer herein.

In my opinion, he is juvenile, puerile, infantile and not very talented at all, although there is a certain adolescent charm to some of his writing. This is surprising, because by all accounts he is an intelligent, 53 year old man, who has held down a responsible job for many years and has a degree in philosophy from a redbrick university.

The problem with this Mike O'Brien is that he has always been a bit of a show off. If he isn't imagining that he is a skilled singer songwriter, he is summoning up the spirit of his dead aunt to convince people of his ability as a clairvoyant. He has even turned his hand to co-writing a musical "Lost in Chuffing Space" which deservedly sank without trace after its first and only performance. And now he is publishing his poetry, an endeavour which he imagines will allow him to take his place amongst the giants of English Literature or the Great British Poets. You have to hand it to him for his optimism.

But don't let me cloud your view. Read on, and see if you truly believe that Mike O'Brien is worthy of ranking alongside the likes of Lord Byron, William Wordsworth and Alexander Pope, or if he should stick to writing on lavatory walls in the future. Only you can decide. And the best of British to you!

1: EAST YORKSHIRE STINKS OF SHIT

East Yorkshire stinks of shit
Get out of Hull towards the coast
The long, flat roads
The plain of Holderness
The rolling Wolds
The scenes that Hockney paints so well
Bigger trees at Warter, Woldgate Woods
All stink of shit

The hum of farm machinery
The crackle of telegraph wires
The silence surrounding it
And the stink of shit

Surrender to it
Breathe it in

Fill your lungs
Good country air
Good, honest shit
Cowshit
Rotting vegetation shit
Filthy, sloppy, muddy shit,
Rainbow patterns in the liquid pools on its surface

Look at it: It will turn your stomach
Taste it: You will gag

But breathe it in, out in that damp East Yorkshire air
When you can already taste the breeze off the North Sea
When you can hear all the small noises cloaked in the silence
Like tiny flies trapped in the head of a pint of bitter
When you smell it out there, the stink of shit is a good, good thing

The smell of boyhood bike rides
Boulder clay cliffs and pebbly beaches
Plastic flotsam from foreign vessels
Crude oil and sand
And good, honest, shit...

2: HOG ROAST

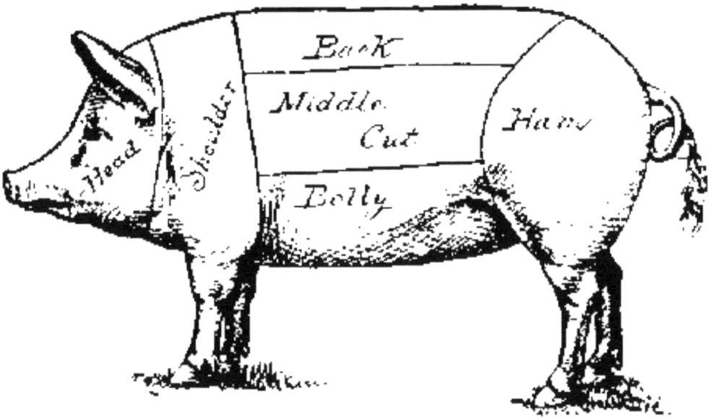

I must admit that I've had better days
Trotting, truffling
Snorting, snuffling
I used to have cloven hooves
I used to have a curly tail
I used to have a sty of my own
Lovers!
Piglets!

I used to enjoy the simple pleasures
Eating,
Sleeping
Farting

For crying out loud!
Look at me now
What am I reduced to?

A sideshow
Skewered and scorched
Sliced for sandwiches
Apple sauce?
Don't mind if I do!

Mind you
Mustn't grumble
Chin up
Keep on smiling
I'll survive

No... I will
I'll live on in all those who munch on my mortal remains
Ingesting the messages stored deep within my DNA
Unlocking
Decoding
Assimilating
Incorporating
Replicating and reproducing

You, my new host
A little less human
A little more porcine
A little less you
A little more me

Evolve?
I don't mind if I do!

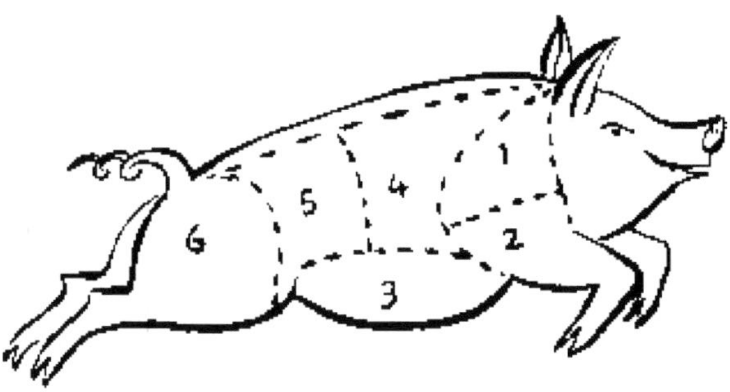

3: THE MACHINE

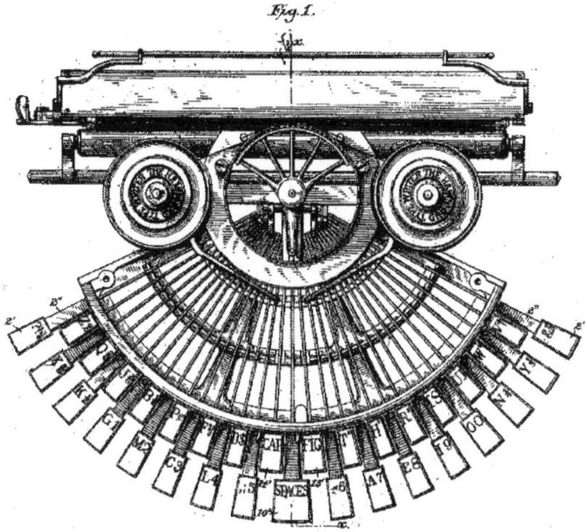

I put my fingers into the machine
A woman in Paris gave me a manicure

I put my hand into the machine
A woman in Singapore gave me a hand massage

I put my arm into the machine
A man in Tokyo gave me a tattoo

I put my arm back into the machine
A surgeon in New York removed the tattoo

I put my foot into the machine
A man in Baltimore trimmed my corns for me

I put my leg into the machine
A man in Debenhams measured it

I put my head into the machine
I man in New Delhi gave me a haircut

I put my whole body into the machine
I was downloaded
And digitised
Into binary
Transcoded
To Hexadecimal
Transcended
Optimised
Cleansed of flesh and bone
Forever

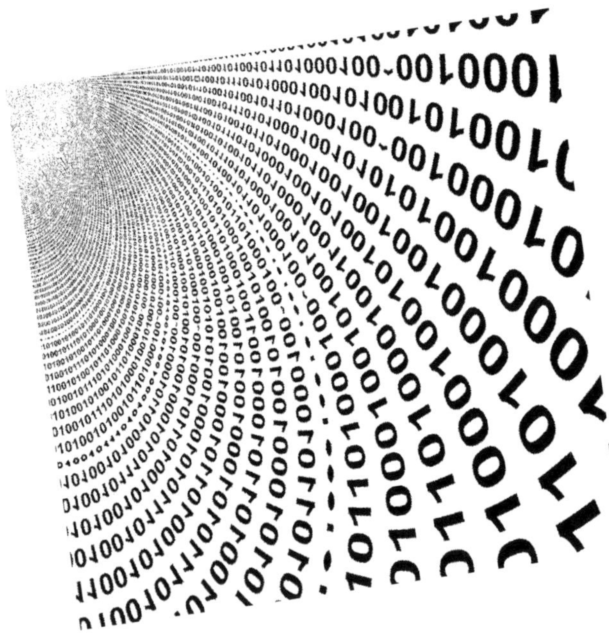

4: THE BRINK OF REVOLUTION

Back in the day when Shakespeare
Was working on a sonnet
He didn't rush the job at all
Spent plenty of time on it
He chose his words dead carefully
Said what he meant to say
And that is why there's lots of folk
Still reading them today

He made a difference
Through poetry
To him, and her and you and you and me
He changed the things that people read
And talk about and think
We're on the brink, of revolution

When Samuel Taylor Coleridge
Was writing Khubla Khan
He never got it finished
Interrupted by a man

But it still inspired people
To pass the story on
Like Frankie Goes to Hollywood
And Olivia Newton John

He made a difference
Through poetry
To him, and her and you and you and me
He changed the things that people read
And talk about and think
We're on the brink, of revolution

When Auden Wrote "The Night Mail"
He was pleased with what he'd done
The Railways and the Royal Mail
Were owned by everyone
Public service industries
The best the world had got
Then greedy Tory bastards came
And privatized the lot

But we make a difference
Through poetry
That's him, and her and you and you and me
We can change the things that people read
And talk about and think
We're on the brink, of revolution

5: LIFETIME ACHIEVEMENT AWARD

I was listening to some Bowie
Laid on my bed the other night
Listening to how Ziggy played the guitar
In the fading evening light
And all that stuff he did with Eno
I was listening to that too
And then I guess I drifted off to sleep
The way you do.
I dreamed that I was David Bowie
At a posh function in New York
Having a Lifetime Achievement award
Presented to me by Bjork

I thanked the cheering audience
I thanked my lovely one time supermodel wife
And I thanked my lucky stars
That I'd had such a wonderful life
What with the magnitude of all that I'd achieved
I felt so proud and tall
Then I woke up and I realised
I wasn't David Bowie at all
I was only Mike O'Brien
And on the table next to me
There was no Lifetime Achievement Award
Just a cold cup of tea

Each one of us spends some time dreaming
Every time we fall asleep
Some of our dreams, they disappear like smoke
And other dreams we keep
Sometimes our dreams seem very, very real
And we believe all that we see
Sometimes we find ourselves completely
Immersed in the reality.
Could it be that I am Bowie?
And Bowie dreams that he is me?
And he has no Lifetime Achievement Award
Just some shit poetry

6: THE TRAMP'S SECRET

Sheltering from the damp of the dawn in a shop doorway
Layer upon layer of clothing for warmth
All filthy
A beard that has been growing for years and years and years
A beard of religious proportions
Like Archbishop Makarios
Like Osama Bin Laden
Like the Lord God Almighty
A beard in nicotine brown,
The same colour as the fingers which poke out of his frayed mittens.
His hair dreadlocked by neglect.
He is fragrant with the aroma of stale tobacco, stale booze, and sun dried piss.

The insect bites don't even itch anymore
His hide is desensitised

He's medicated against disease and depression by a 7% ABV preparation of factory produced cider, delivered in regular 3 litre doses.

So why does he look so happy this morning?
What's his secret?
Do you really want to know?

Well...

Beneath his filthy raiment,
Inside his ragged, stinking drawers
Is a God given hard on.
Independent of anticipation or recollection
Not born of conscious desire or lustful thought
Unaided by pornography, medication or manual stimulation
As pure and natural as the sunlight
As solid as an oaken bough
Bursting with life

It doesn't matter if you are a flea bitten tramp taking shelter in a shop doorway.
The president of the United States of America
Or the Dali fucking Llama
Whoever you are
A hard on like that feels just as bloody marvellous!

7: GAGGING

I'm gagging for a fag
And there's nowt wrong with that
They keep you healthy
They keep you alert
They relax you
Keep you social
Keep your mind on the game
Clear your pipes

It's only natural
Tobacco
Full of flavour
It's the chemicals they add to it that causes the damage

It's warm inside the smoking shelter
Makes you feel warm inside
Companionship
Friendship

All my friends are dead
Ashes to ashes

It's warm inside the smoking shelter
A great big outdoor heater

A glowing top
A glowing tip
Orange heat
Brown fingertips
Stale filter tips
Ashes to ashes

In through the mouth and out through the nose
Or blowing rings with round mouthed puffs
In the living room at home
Watching the curling blue smoke
Ascending in shafts of sunlight

That ceiling was white when I painted it
I used to bound up those stairs
I used to love the aroma of fresh mown grass
I used to be a magnet for the lasses
They used to be gagging for it
I used to be gagging for it

Now?
I'm just gagging for a fag
And there's nowt wrong with that.

8: TOMBOLA

325 wins you some ginger snaps
Select ginger snaps

125 wins you some Nivea
Sensitive Nivea, for men

175 wins you some bodywash and lotion
Crabtree and Evelyn bodywash and lotion
50ml of each
In a presentation box

245 wins you some post it notes
Disguised as a slice of melon
"Fruit Notes"
Made in China

Outside the village hall
A grey English sky
A stone wall
A stiff breeze

365 wins you some ladies handkerchiefs
Lavender and almond blossom

85 wins you some lip balm
Beeswax lip balm

45 wins you some hand and nail cream
Sensual hand and nail cream
Blended with pure essential oil of damask rose

165 wins you a salt pot and a pepper pot
In the shape of two embracing figures

Around the room, the ladies and their husbands
Exchanging money
Raising funds
For cancer

9: OH HO HO HO, CARL DOUGLAS

Oh ho ho ho, Carl Douglas, In August '74
You were number one in the Hit Parade
And you'd not been there before
Thursday night on Top of the Pops
It must have been so damn exciting
Watching everybody getting on down
To your song about Kung Fu Fighting

Oh ho ho ho, Carl Douglas,
A Jamaican reggae man
Got into funk and rock and roll
When you came to Eng-er-land
Jammed on stage with Hendrix
At a concert in Crouch End
And counted Johnny Guitar Watson
As a personal friend

Oh ho ho ho Johnny Guitar Watson
A big influence on Etta James
And various other American legends
But I can't recall their names
I know... I digress... I'm sorry
I don't want to bore ya
But he did have a minor UK hit,
With "A Real Mother For Ya"

Oh ho ho ho Carl Douglas
In October '74
Everyone who had bought your record
Was wanting something more
Crunch time! Now's the chance
To show what you can really do
But you blew it big time when you released
"Dancing the Kung Fu"

Oh ho ho ho Carl Douglas
Where did it all go wrong?
Now the only thing you're remembered for
Is that bloody stupid song

10: THAT'S WHY I LIKE YOU

I could try and fit in if I put in the effort.
I could learn to tell the difference between Leone and Rhianna
And Christina Aguilera
And their ilk

I could learn which ones were x factor finalists
Or x factor guests or x factor judges
I could gossip about who they were seeing
Who they were sleeping with,
Who they were staying awake with
I could learn all of that stuff, but it wouldn't be me

I could try and fit in if I put in the effort
I could learn the difference between a Seat Ibiza
And a Vauxhall Corsa
I could teach myself to care that they are not as desirable
As a Hyundai Santa Fe
Or one of those trucks with Animal written on the side
I could learn to speak with authority on
Diesel v unleaded v super plus unleaded
I could make jokes about fuel injection
And electro petrochemical hybrids

And smartphones, and headphones,
And social networks and tablets and apps
And 78inch "high definition" screens
With blu ray plug and play internet ready ways and means
Of watching movies and features and soaps and music vids
With Leone and Rhianna and Christine Aguilera
And their ilk

I could take a list of celebrities long as my arm
Longer even
I could learn all their names
I could learn all about them

As if they were my friends
My family
My confidantes
I could learn all about all of that stuff
But it wouldn't be me

I could learn all the premier league football talk,
United and City and Villa and Palace
And who sponsors the shirts
And who is injured
And who is selected to play for their country and
And who has transferred to where
And which manager is for the sack
And which player was seen out at a nightclub,
Being sick through their nose
All over Leone
All over Rhianna
All over Christina Aguilera
And their ilk

I could learn all that stuff
I could try and fit in
I could train myself to take an interest
But it wouldn't be me.
And it wouldn't be you either.

But what about all the stuff that I think IS me
And all the stuff that you think IS you
The Tarantino and the Clash
The indie bands and the funny hats
The swearing
The joking
The tattoos the piercings
The weird beards
The sub culture culture
That's oh so much better
Than what's in the tabloids

Oh so much better
Than what they try to sell us
We're better
Way better
We have quirky tics
That set us apart

But anyone could learn all that
If they put in the effort
If they wanted to fit in
With the crowd that we're in
But it wouldn't be them
It isn't even me
It isn't even you.
It isn't us at all

We could lose the lot
We WILL lose the lot
Forget it all
In an instant
Or slowly
Don't worry
It isn't us
It isn't us at all
There's more to you and me than all that

And deep, deep down
Below the level of labels and gadgets
Below the level of throwaway likes and dislikes
Below the level of thissing and thatting
And cheap definitions
You know it too
And that's why I like you

11: SMILING VICTORIANS

We are the smiling Victorians
We went against the grain
We rebelled against stiff, starchy seriousness
Frock coated frumpery
And mutton jowled misery
We are the cheerful subjects of Albert's widow

Some of us are children, who smile naturally
Some of us are adults
Who, common wisdom suggests, should know better
Than to smile into a lens
Without modesty

They say that a smile is like an ankle
Or even a calf
That only someone close
Should be allowed to gaze upon it
Not a thing to be photographed
And exposed to the stares of all and sundry

But we say:
Smile
Look at my smile
Smile back at me
Let it happen
Dissolve the starch
Soften eyes and cheeks
Lose yourself in the response

There

That's better, isn't it.

12: STEVE PEREGRIN TOOK

Steve Peregrin Took
Had a charming English hippie look
That English hippie lasses found appealing
When he travelled up and down the land
As the bongo man in Bolan's band
He pulled more birds than Bolan did
And Bolan hit the ceiling

And the people of the Beltane
And the Dworns were all dismayed
And the king of the Rumbling Spires
Decreed that solemn music played
When Bolan said (Hey Hey)

Steve Peregrin Took
You'll have to sling your hook
I'm replacing you with a man called Mickey Finn
And now I'll get more birds because
The lasses will not care a toss
For Mickey because Mickey is as hideous as sin

And Stacey Grove (who was a nice guy)
Locked himself away
And the Children of the Rarn
Refrained from frolic, song and play
That fateful day (Hey Hey)

When Steve Peregrin Took
Gave Bolan a withering look
And formed new bands to play the songs he wrote
He was in Pink Fairies and Shagrat
And Steve Took's Horns and bands like that
But then he choked to death
With a cocktail cherry
Stuck in his drug numbed throat.

Saint Peter and The Lord both smiled
When Took and Bolan reconciled
In the eternal kingdom high
They played some great gigs in the sky
And when death came to Mickey Finn
They gladly asked him to join in
For up in heaven (as they found)
There's plenty birds to go around

13: WHEN I AM PISSED[1]

When I am pissed
Conspiracy theories
Metaphysics
Quantum physics
The multiverse
Particles travelling forwards and backwards through time
Are all appealing
All make sense

I know that there are other drugs
More efficient
At liberating the mind
But look at me
They are illegal
And I look more like a copper
Than a drug user
I have a middle class life
Booze is easily and cheaply available

What was Tony Blair playing at?
Declaring war on Iran?
What was David Icke on about?
Shell suited Messiah?
When I am pissed
I understand

[1] This was actually written whilst I was pissed!

14: DELUSIONS OF GRANDEUR

Sir Paul McCartney called me on the telephone
And said, Mike would you like to come to tea
With the Mrs and me
And Bryan Ferry
It will be very, very good
Hop on a train to Liverpool
I'll meet you at the station at about a half past three
We'll get on tremendously
So I hopped on a train to Liverpool
And I was waiting at the station at twenty past three
And twenty past four
And five o'clock came and went before I realised
I've never even spoken to Sir Paul
At all
Ever in my life
It was just my Delusions of Grandeur

Doctor Nikki Alexander out of Silent Witness
Asked me if I wanted to be her Facebook friend
She said it didn't have to end
On Facebook
With a little bit of luck
I could go down to her laboratory
And we could do autopsies together
Friends Forever
So I went to buy a ticket to her place
Then I realised that I didn't know where her place was
And that she didn't exist
And she looks like Edward Fox out of "Day of the Jackal"
Which isn't too surprising as she is his daughter
I aughter
Know by now
It was just my Delusions of Grandeur

The all powerful creator of the Universe
Spoke to me inside my head
Whilst I was in bed
He Said
I have selected you to be
The messiah of the 21st century
Tell everyone where they are going wrong
Perhaps in song
So I told everyone I was the chosen one
Explained to them where they were going wrong
In song
But I was ridiculed and scorned before I realised
I wasn't any sort of a Messiah at all
I felt so small
And foolish

It was just my Delusions of Grandeur again
Just some rogue neurons and chemistry
Screwing up my brain
They had me for a while there
They really jerked my chain
Delusions of Grandeur again.

15: PANIC

Ohh God
Got to breathe
Got to calm down
Got to relax
Got to go back in and act normal
No one will ever know it was me
No one saw me going in
No one saw me coming out

I didn't know I had it in me
It was just too big to flush away
I got rid of the little ones
I got rid of the paper
I flushed twice
But the big one…
There was nothing in there to poke it or slice it with
I suppose it will dissolve in time
Probably
Possibly
Maybe

What more could I do?
Confess?
No one need ever know
It could have been anybody
Anybody male
How many men work here?
Four?
Five?
Six including me

Only...
The one who discovers it will know that HE didn't do it
Five suspects then
Unless.....
Unless he didn't look before he sat down
He might THINK that he did it
Did I look before I sat down?
Maybe not
But I KNOW it was me
I felt it coming out

Ohh God
I'll DIE if it comes out
If anyone says anything
They'll KNOW I'm guilty
I'll blush
I'll sweat
They'll smell it on me
Fear
Guilt

Wish I had stayed home
But I didn't
Got to take a deep breath
Go back in
Act Normal

16: INNARDS

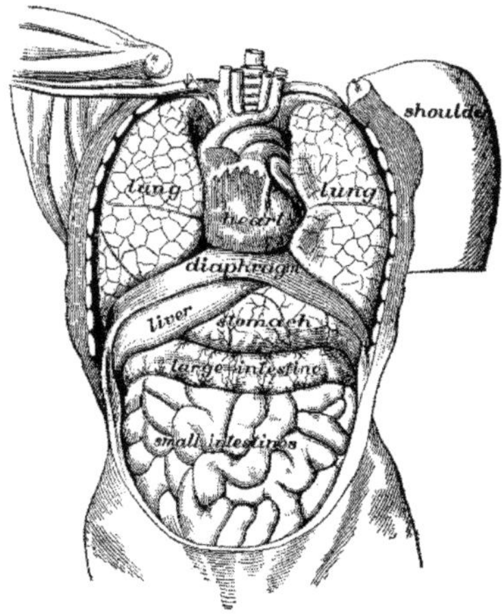

It was the dead of night
I was in bed
I was laid on my side
I was comfortable
But then...
My innards started to complain...

"We're not comfy
We're all squished to one side
Maybe if you rolled over
Turned the other way
Then we would be able to get comfy
Aww... Go on...
Please"

They wouldn't shut up
So I rolled over
But...
Just as I was getting comfortable once more
Just as I was drifting off
My innards started up again

"We're still not comfy
Well... we were for a bit
But we're aren't any more
We're all squished to the other side now
Maybe if you rolled over
And lay on your stomach
Maybe we could get comfy then...
Aww... Go on
Please...
Pretty Please"

I could tell that they were not going to shut up unless I did
So I rolled over onto my stomach
And relaxed...
And my body got heavier
And my thoughts drifted away
And I was almost asleep
When....
Those innards were at it again

"We're still not comfy
Well... We were
But we're all pressed into your ribs now
We're all squished together
We're getting sore
You could roll over onto your back
We would be comfy then
Go on....
Pretty, Pretty Please"

So I rolled over onto my back
And got comfortable
And started to drift
And float away
But...
Inevitably
My sodding innards started up again

"We're still not comfy..."
"RIGHT!" I said
"THAT'S ENOUGH" I said
I LEAPT out of bed
I RAN to the bathroom, knelt down and
GRASPED the toilet bowl with both hands and
I HURLED my innards
Out of my mouth and into the basin
Heart, Lungs, Liver, Kidneys, Intestines, Gall Bladders
Everything from my neck to my hips.
All out
In a whoosh of colour
A torrent of fizzing and dripping giblets
A slithering, sliding, slippery succession of vital organs
Screaming, shouting and shrieking as they shot out of me

"Whoooargh!
Steady on!
Ruddy Norah
Whoooooooargh!"

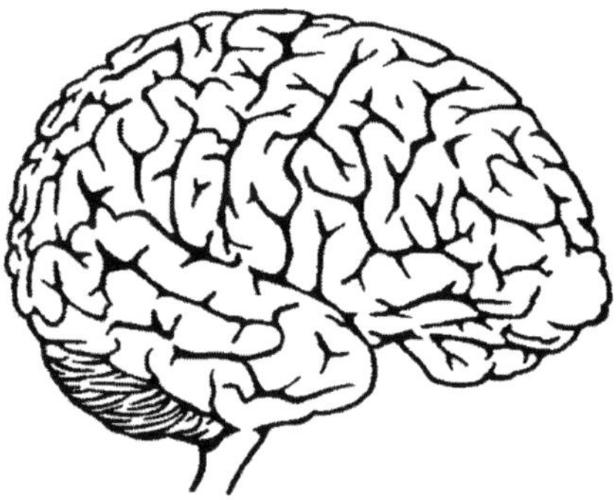

Then
With a hollow rib cage
With an empty middle
With nothing left to give
I tottered back to bed
I lay down
I relaxed
I got comfortable
And as my consciousness finally left me
My brain said
"Thank god that lot have gone
We can finally get some sleep"

The illustration of a brain on this page is actually a maze! Can you get from the spinal column to the frontal lobes without crossing a line?

17: WATCHING THE TRIMMERS

When we were thirteen
Or maybe fourteen
We all had paper rounds
Me and Lee Henson
And Michael Courtney
In Trimmer's Newsagents
With Mr Trimmer
Who was a misery

We used to laugh behind his back
When he got cross with us because
We'd pushed a paper through the letterbox
Next door to where it should have gone
And some bloke rang up to complain
Because he hadn't seen the Sun
To read at breakfast time and fill
His mind with utter shite before
He had to leave the house
So that he could get himself in to work on time

Old Mister Trimmer
What a misery
He didn't pay us much
He made us work hard
He never cracked a smile
Nor did his Mrs
So they seemed suited
To each other

We would wait in the back room
For the newspapers to arrive
And we'd pinch chocolate from his stock
When he went in the front to serve
And on the evening we would climb
Over his garden wall and lie

Down in the bushes and observe
His feet and Mrs Trimmer's feet
Because the curtains on his French windows
Didn't quite reach all the way down to the floor

Why did we do that?
It used to make us laugh
But it was innocent
Just like we were
We thought the other kids
All had girlfriends
And we had no-one
So we watched Trimmer

Then one day he started being kind
He gave us all a pay rise and
He even gave us chocolate
So we didn't have to pinch it
And then shortly after that
Old Trimmer died and went to heaven
So his Mrs closed the shop and
Me, Lee Henson and Mike Courtney
Found ourselves without a job
And so we had to find new paper rounds elsewhere.

18: THEM

First, they came for the sugar
And I did not speak out
Because I do not take sugar in tea or coffee

Then they came for the flour,
And I remained silent
Because I usually have a sliced loaf from Morrisons

Then they came for the eggs
And still I said nothing.
I am not particularly fond of eggs.

Then they came for tea
And I was unable to bake a cake
Because all the ingredients were gone.

19: LOVE, SEX & POWER PETE

Long haired Pete, hippie Pete
Peace and Understanding Pete
Pete lives on pasta
Thin and pale
Pete CND
Pete save the whale

Bearded Pete
Pete corduroy
Tolkien Pete
Such a nice boy
Pete velvet loons
Pete Jesus boots
Pete stars and moons
Pete bells and flutes

Hippie shop
Pete's always in
Sells incense stick
And baccy tin
Ciggy papers, extra long
Grinders, pipes and water bong

That was the shop where Pete had been
The day he bought that magazine
Counter culture magazine
Underground, the hippie scene
Weave your own mat
Fat Freddie's cat
And other stuff to read like that

And plenty more
Page twenty four
An advert made him stop
Say "Cor!"

The Key To
LOVE, SEX AND POWER
Revealed
3 Day Residential Retreat in the Yorkshire Dales
Unlock your potential
Learn how to draw
LOVE, SEX AND POWER
To yourself
Box No 3549: Goole

Pete got in touch
Pete got a place
It put a smile
Upon Pete's face
Pete went one Friday on a train
Never to be seen again

Next Monday, someone new to meet
Love and Sex and Power Pete!

He'd had a shave
He'd cut his hair
All we could do was stand and stare
At leather shoes
At denim jeans
A smart but casual man of means

Pete glinting eye
Pete knowing look
Pete transformed by that course he took
Pete chat up lasses
Pete the lad
Pete the bounder
Pete the cad

Pete motorcycle
Pete risk taker
Pete the mover
Pete the shaker

Friends in high places
Weekends golfing
Pete eat tuna
Sod the dolphin

Pete older now
Married with kids
Pete never do
What wife forbids
Mortgage Pete
Pete rat race man
Pete slave to wage
Pete pension plan
Fond memories of
That golden hour
The time Pete had
Love, Sex and Power.

20: ANYONE CAN DO IT NOWADAYS

When someone says they have a deal
For publishing their book
It probably means nothing
I wouldn't give a fuck
Anyone can do it nowadays

And if they say their publisher
Was recently in touch
I wouldn't get excited
It doesn't mean that much
Anyone can do it nowadays

Its not even expensive
To get stuff into print
Any silly sod can do it
Any stupid bint
Anyone can do it nowadays

Ohh its coming out on Kindle?
Well goodness gracious me
I wouldn't get excited
We can all do that for free.

Of course its hard to do all that
Formatting and that writing
But the publishers don't care
If you just send a load of shite in

They never really read it
Before they print it out
And no-one reads it after
So its nowt to shout about
Anyone can do it nowadays

So the next time someone shows you
Their latest book, you should
Resist the urge to be impressed
Unless its any good
Anyone can do it nowadays

THE END

AFTERWORD

All About Me

Although Professor Iain Duncan Norville is a figment of my imagination, much of what he said in the introduction is true. I have been three pop groups who have all failed to gain any popular recognition. The Z Men were a noisy teenage punk band, in which I gave up my Yorkshire accent to sound cockney. The Velvetones were a sort of swing meets pop eighties band, which fed into the Housemartins and the Beautiful South, leaving me behind, and my current group, Pocketful O'Nowt, are just as immature as both of the other ones.
You can find out about stuff like that if you poke around here…

www.nowtnet.com

I also do some clairvoyant comedy and a lot of writing whilst under the influence of my dear departed Auntie Doris.
You can find out about Doris here…

auntdoris.wordpress.com

This is my first attempt at vanity publishing. I wouldn't be so vain if I could get anyone interested in publishing my other projects. A book of songs, and two books by Auntie Doris, featuring her life story and her guide to the tarot.

Cheers

Mike O'Brien
zoomburst@gmail.com

17179125R00031

Printed in Great Britain
by Amazon